Science and Other Poems

SCIENCE AND OTHER POEMS

ALISON HAWTHORNE DEMING

LOUISIANA STATE UNIVERSITY PRESS
Baton Rouge and London

1994

Manufactured in the United States of America
First printing
03 02 01 00 99 98 97 96 95 94   5 4 3 2 1
Designer: Amanda McDonald Key
Typeface: Sabon
Typesetter: G & S Typesetters, Inc.
Printer and binder: Thomson–Shore, Inc.

Library of Congress Cataloging-in-Publication Data

Deming, Alison Hawthorne, 1946–
     Science and other poems / Alison Hawthorne Deming.
          p.   cm.
     ISBN 0-8071-1914-8 (cl).—ISBN 0-8071-1915-6 (p)
     I. Title.
PS3554.E474S35   1994
811'.54—dc20

93-39187
CIP

The author offers grateful acknowledgment to the magazines that originally published these poems, many in different versions: *Beloit Poetry Journal* (Summer, 1983), "The Woman Painting Crates"; *Black Warrior Review* (Fall, 1984), "The Stone Breakers"; *Calliope* (May, 1984), "Dreamwork with Horses," "Snapshots for My Daughter"; *Crazyhorse* (Spring, 1991), "Caffe Trieste," "Shakers"; *Cumberland Poetry Review* (Fall, 1984), "Dreamwork," "Eve Revisited," "From Away," "The Gardener," "North"; *Denver Quarterly Review* (Fall, 1980), "Island Stars"; *Hayden's Ferry Review* (Spring, 1993), "Camp Tontozona"; *Kennebec*, "Breading the Soft-Shelled Crabs"; *Michigan Quarterly Review* (Spring, 1985), "Fiber Optics and the Heart"; *Newsletter of the Poetry Society of America* (Summer, 1992), "Twin Falls"; *Nimrod* (Fall, 1983), "Letter to Nathaniel Hawthorne"; *Penumbra* (3rd/4th Quarter, 1980), "Stuck for Repairs in Tucson"; *Portland Review of the Arts* (April, 1982), "Canoeing the Salt Marsh," (Spring, 1984), "Saturday, J.'s Oyster Bar"; *Provincetown Arts* (1993), "Searching for the Lost," (1991), "Staying over Nature"; *Rhetoric Review* (Winter, 1991), "At the Hairdresser's I Think of Heraclitus"; *Sequoia* (Summer, 1988), "First Encounter Beach"; *Shankpainter* (Spring, 1985), "Breakwater," "Refuge," (Spring, 1987), "Grand Manan," (Spring, 1989), "Off-Season"; *Tendril* (Winter, 1984), "Bells." "Science" and "My Intention" first appeared in *The Uncommon Touch: Poetry and Fiction from the Stanford Writing Program* (Stanford, 1989). "The Russians" first appeared in *The Eloquent Edge: 15 Maine Women Writers* (Bar Harbor, Maine, 1990).

The author is particularly thankful for the Fine Arts Work Center in Provincetown, the Stegner Fellowship Program at Stanford University, the Corporation of Yaddo, Cummington Community for the Arts, and the Djerassi Foundation for the support and friendships that helped her complete this work. Appreciation, as well, goes to the National Endowment for the Arts for a 1990 Literature Fellowship.

*For my mother, Travilla Macnab Deming
and in memory of my father, Benton Hawthorne Deming*

CONTENTS

I

Science / 3
Twin Falls / 5
Caffe Trieste / 7
The Stone Breakers / 8
Canoeing the Salt Marsh / 9
Shooting Flamingoes / 11
Refuge / 12
Breakwater / 13
Fiber Optics and the Heart / 14
North / 15
Año Nuevo / 16
At the Ranch / 18
Grand Manan / 20
Letter to Nathaniel Hawthorne / 22
The Dream of a Moral Life / 27

II

First Encounter Beach / 31
Bells / 33
Breading the Soft-Shelled Crabs / 34
At the Hairdresser's I Think of Heraclitus / 35
Eve Revisited / 36
Dreamwork / 37
From Away / 38
Stuck for Repairs in Tucson / 39
The Massage / 40
Saturday, J.'s Oyster Bar / 41
Shakers / 42
Reception / 43
Snapshots for My Daughter / 44
Scenes from Childhood / 45
    How We Did It / 45
    Seven / 47
    Alliance, Ohio / 48
    Museum Piece / 49
    The Pelican / 50

III

Mt. Lemmon, Steward Observatory, 1990 / 53
My Intention / 57
The Woman Painting Crates / 58
Island Stars / 60
Camp Tontozona / 61
Dreamwork with Horses / 63
Off-Season / 65
The Russians / 66
Instructions on, *Or Rather,* Examples
    of How to Love the Earth / 67
The Gardener / 68
Recital / 69
The Man Who Became a Deer / 70
At the Marin Exhibit / 72
Searching for the Lost / 73
Letter to Michael / 74
Staying over Nature / 76

Science and Other Poems

I

SCIENCE

Then it was the future, though what's arrived
isn't what we had in mind, all chrome and
cybernetics, when we set up exhibits
in the cafeteria for the judges
to review what we'd made of our hypotheses.

The class skeptic (he later refused to sign
anyone's yearbook, calling it a sentimental
degradation of language) chloroformed mice,
weighing the bodies before and after
to catch the weight of the soul,

wanting to prove the invisible
real as a bagful of nails. A girl
who knew it all made cookies from euglena,
a one-celled compromise between animal and plant,
she had cultured in a flask.

We're smart enough, she concluded,
to survive our mistakes, showing photos of farmland,
poisoned, gouged, eroded. No one believed
he really had built it when a kid no one knew
showed up with an atom smasher, confirming that

the tiniest particles could be changed
into something even harder to break.
And one whose mother had cancer (hard to admit now,
it was me) distilled the tar of cigarettes
to paint it on the backs of shaven mice.

She wanted to know what it took,
a little vial of sure malignancy,
to prove a daily intake smaller
than a single aspirin could finish
something as large as a life. I thought of this

because, today, the dusky seaside sparrow
became extinct. It may never be as famous
as the pterodactyl or the dodo,
but the last one died today, a resident
of Walt Disney World where now its tissue samples

lie frozen, in case someday we learn to clone
one from a few cells. Like those instant dinosaurs

that come in a gelatin capsule—just add water
and they inflate. One other thing this
brings to mind. The euglena girl won first prize

both for science and, I think, in retrospect, for hope.

TWIN FALLS

Evening. The reservoir rimmed with tattered
rain-pocked cliffs, graffiti sand-blasted off
leaving ghostly remains of the town's self-abuse
(rural version—painted white). Above the falls
children swim or play with cartoon buckets.

"Don't put your fishes in that water,"
a father says to the kid with the sky-blue net
trying to spoon his minnows into a jug of tapwater.
"They'll die in there. It's too purified."

Tomorrow I'll cross Massacre Rocks, the Lost River Sinks
and, rimmed in the atlas by a jagged pink band,
the Idaho National Atomic Energy Reservation
where my friend almost worked after fine-tuning his nerves

lowering the reactor into the first nuclear sub.
By the time I met him, he'd given up engineering,
the Porsche and martinis. The problem wasn't technology,
he claimed, but people who couldn't be trusted.

A strawberry-blond braid rivered between his shoulder blades.
Cranked on caffeine, or whatever substance had biked into town,
he mixed sound for a band, lived in a ramshackle sawmill
where he tinkered mostly with the idea

of retooling the waterfall to generate
power for the dozen of us, urban refugees,
who were reclaiming those failed farms and schools.
Why do I say "reclaim" when they weren't ours to start with—
we'd just found bargains in a stranger's loss.

Twin Falls. It's the summer of a heatwave
that's burned out more farms,
the summer pilots found a hole in the sky.
Shop windows papered with "QUITTING" signs,
the only bar doing business named "Escape."

Nothing's rolling over the falls—what water
hasn't been diverted upstream
to grow the nation's hottest potatoes
pools in the reservoir where farmers and bankers,
Native and Christian, swim until dark.

The aluminum diving board bangs as
one cool body after another
pulls arm over arm toward the raft.

CAFFE TRIESTE

American experience . . . so often is grief disguised as plenitude.
                                    —*W. S. Di Piero*

It's too hot for April and the recycled Hawaiian shirts
for sale on Grant Street cost fifty bucks.
I hate the way the past gets turned into marketing—
the fifties now chrome walls fanning over formica,
polished until they look as if no one ever ate a cracker there,

and the waitresses wearing caps shaped like take-out french fry containers.
They're not the fifties when bombs spread like bacteria on culture plates,
when the cost of a family staying together might be Stelazine and
high-voltage erasures. They're just American—all shine and no pain.

Grant Street—a crowd spills out of the Caffe Trieste,
accordion music and a woman singing arias that make bystanders weep.
It's not just her singing, says one who's stood long in the sidewalk's heat.
It's the way she delivers—a swaggering Carmen slapping down
the empty wineglass in a boast, the way she shakes her head

at the close of the high note as if coming up from a muscular dive.
Then the man who stands with a portable mike near the door,
not particularly well-dressed or theatrical, but charming,
cuts an aisle through the tables, setting her up for the harmony
the audience wants to feel, announcing—*My daughter*—more surprised

than the bystanders who walked past vintage shops, windows
dressed with roped-up salami and the new formalism of pasta,
to find that these sounds could come from anyone's body—much less
bone of my bone—songs of passion and cruelty
reaching in to a place that wants to let loose.

THE STONE BREAKERS

The rough-hewn boy is young for roadwork.
Bracing a tub of picked stones to his knee

he daydreams a target for each one. At his age
nothing fits—the hand-me-down outgrown trousers,

the job that goes on like the bother of gnats, or the old man
dislodging the chert and the quartzite, whose mattock is so small

he works on his knees, his back
worn to a permanent slump from making do.

Plain faceless people—they don't look up
from the jumbled igneous crop

as they smooth and widen the way
for the salon-going society of Paris

who will no doubt complain that the canvas
is too coarse, too large, mere brutalities

of color daubed with a knife. *Show me an angel
and I'll paint one,* Courbet will boast

strutting, truculent, in the Pavilion of Realism.
This painting, lost during world war, transmits

by its absence the new sense of the real.
The man and the boy, too old and too young

to take sides, were freed from the frame and the tireless
tasting of the middle-class—like horses unharnessed

they shook off their work, drank in
the shade of the nearest oak and broke wind.

CANOEING THE SALT MARSH
Scarborough, Maine

All eels migrate to the Sargasso
to breed, the guide says, dragging
fingers like a seine behind the canoe
to catch the feel of the tidal stream,
sense the shimmer of a species
coming together in January.

July now. Last year's offspring
lounge under mats of algae,
filter the peat-flecked stream
through gills and wait to be stirred.

Blades glisten in the sanctuary.

Osprey. Black-back. Herring gull.

Scanning the tapestry of greens,
I want to know the one grass
that survives by extruding salt
along its glittering spine.
Bivalves too adapt. Submerged
three days in sterile tanks,
they pump themselves clean of coliform,
then leave the stocky Blue Point factory—
sweet, minced, and canned.

The Penobscots came to that point,
dug and dried clams enough
to last the inland winter
that tucked them underneath the scrubby pines.

Their sanctuary was endless.

Jackpine, jack rabbit, jack-in-the-pulpit,

where now the subdivided county
sleeps outside the fence
that keeps the salt marsh safe,
SAC planes overhead
drag thunder through the perfect sky.

Moving with the outgoing tide,
flotsam of microbes and mica-lit sand, moving
toward the prayer that everything is praying,
I wake up with the eels at the blood-call.

SHOOTING FLAMINGOES

Brazil. The salt marsh, a dried slime in summer
which no other creature abides. They rise in columns
from the grid of cones—mud-packed nests
that honeycomb across the dull green.
The painter thins pigment to dry quickly,

unrolling the canvas while regiments
still climb from the nests,
the heads of young birds gawking out,
pink so dim as to look like a smudge.
Six or eight lie dead, necks lopped,
legs akimbo. Others hobble under broken wings.

The guide, fallen in the willow blind,
raises a black hand in caution. The painter,
commissioned by Colt Firearms, positions himself
in the foreground, a counterweight to the birds
propelled like javelins out of the scene.

He aims "Sam"—named for its maker—
at the leading bird and blares off,
smoke and fire echoing the same
titanium and cadmium as wings, beaks, and breasts.

Maybe it never happened this way. But that's how
he painted it. And why include, exactly above
the gunblast, the snow-clad peaks of the Andes,
if not to tell he knew the higher ground.

—*after George Catlin*

REFUGE

Glossy ibis, says the guide, setting her tripod
on pavement, training the lens for the birdwatchers
to fix the downward curved bill and spindly legs
of the wader. I can't help but itch
to get closer than this tailored birdwalk. Once

I rode to low marshland with a friend. The horses
mucking up to their knees, parting the brushy alders
where there wasn't any trail. We gave them their heads,
trusting their instincts to get to dry land.
On the far side we rested, the woods

glowing with rust and lemon. We sat. Reins dropped,
the horses leaned to fidget the leaves.
Wind thickened in the evergreens. Then the quiet cracked—
wings that loud slapped the air—brittle legs
arrowed through weeds to land not five feet away.

The great blue heron, eye fired toward shore,
where we held our breath. Even when
we began to speak, edging slightly closer,
she stayed. And something in her lack of fear,
the fix of one black iris on us—horses,

woman and man alike—kept us in our place.

BREAKWATER

The fisherman pulls a wad of rockweed
from his plastic bread sack, unthreading
sandworms from the tangle. The bay shines
like the skin of a bluefish and he waits.

He waits for the flounder and when it comes
he waits for the next flounder. They flip
in the bucket, half dead. He's glad
to tip back his visor, sitting on the granite blocks

that keep the city at bay. What if right now
his wife walks deliberately into traffic.
What if one car does what she can't
do for herself. He doesn't know it,

he doesn't have to care. He just keeps
slipping the bristly bait on the hook.
He just keeps waiting for the slow biters to come.

FIBER OPTICS AND THE HEART

When a man dies
lights go on
in the theater.
The lens-tipped wand
threads the ventricle
exposing a web
of glistening cords
that tie down
the tricuspid valve
which funnels spent blood
toward revival. The filament
passes wet tabs of muscle
that channel clean blood
from the atrium
to the semi-lunar valves,
membranes shaped like teacups
that portion the flow
down the red-walled tunnel
to the junction of iliac arteries.
Here the passage divides
to replenish pelvis and legs,
the fork diffusing light
like the mouth of a cave
seen from within,
so that the wand reaches
back to the walls of Lascaux
where painting the bull's
charcoal head
kept the hunter alive
by capturing first
the image
of what could kill
or sustain.

NORTH

Morning. The dark horses
absorb sunlight, sheep
graze fast as fall shrinks

the feast, time unhomogenized
by doing twice-daily chores—
feeding salt in the heat,

molasses in the cold—not missing
the moment when you go into
the barn in a snowstorm,

the sky does a quick grey-to-blue
and you come out to maple trees,
weed stalks, even the barbed-wire fence

wearing a thin skin of ice.
Seen at just the right angle,
the sunlight fires that skin to gold,

just for a moment, before clouds
crowd in and even with the stove
stoked full you'll be cold for hours

but not really mind. The old neighbor
saws all winter by hand—
body stiff as wood, bending slow

to the sawhorse, baling twine
hanging from porch rafters in loops
the size of muskrat legs.

Summers—he milks his cow
right in the pasture
and she doesn't walk away.

AÑO NUEVO

A man with four children
crowding like saplings around him
whistles to wake up
the elephant seal who has hulked
his impossible body onto the beach.

A loser, says the egghead kid. The winners
herd onto the Point with females and mate.

Cameras, scopes, and tripods.
And the seal sleeps, his buried heart
rippling the surface of his flesh
like something beginning to boil.
He sleeps on his face. His snout
flaps against the sand when he snores,
shapeless neck wearing
the crusted garland of blood.

He doesn't move when the occasional wave
washes around him. A breathing rock.

People come down the beach
with their red plaids and pink stripes.
A woman walks six inches from the collapsed
warrior without looking. They want the animal
to acknowledge them, to care
as much about the human presence
as they care about his. They want him to ripple up
monstrous out of his torpor so they
can run back to safety, laughing.

Sometimes a tremor will pass
along his length as if to shake off
the body's necessities.
The surf is a white cuff
trimming the placid ocean and the right-angled
cliffs glisten with buttery sunlight.
The picnics continue, the cameras, and hawks.

Now a white-haired docent arrives,
draws with his presence
a circle twenty-feet wide.
Even so, some still need reminding.

Now the side flipper
stretches up, its hand flexing
as the creature sighs deeper into sleep,
the combat falling from his mind.

AT THE RANCH

This morning Apricot and Balzac bantered
over a dead rabbit, the dominant tabby
winning out, tossing the kill
in the playful way of predators.
It's how they learn the skill—
flipping the little carcass in the air
batting it like an empty can—
prelude to the feast when
our domestic cuddle thing
hunkers down and starting
with the head consumes the catch—
ears, entrails, thumper feet, and all.

Witnessing this, I think that humans
ought to trace their genes
back to plants—tasseled grasses
singing the wind, modulating
as the season turns them brown.
Or the horsetail, sporophytic Methusaleh
surviving since the Carboniferous—
its jointed stalks and whorls of leaf
tree-sized in those days when amphibians
slithered in the green gloom beneath
gigantic ferns and club moss,
when insects three-feet wide
droned the steamy deltas, a landscape
not yet capable of mammals or of birds.

But it's not enough to imagine
predating the dinosaurs and outlasting
the Crusades—three hundred million years
of right decisions and the horsetail's
now a knee-high weed, meadows of it
humming dumbly on the forest floor.
Easier to identify with that recent
ancient murrelet—Pacific seabird
stranded in the Bristol Channel—
which drew hundreds of Britons to gawk and
speculate how she could have gotten
so far off the migratory track.
If she could talk she'd beg them—
Quit the gawking and help me back to my kind.

For us, there's no one watching
but the dead, who wish they *could*
lift us from our drifting and
ship us to the habitat where our moves
would be sure, and our language—
every coo and shriek—more sure.

GRAND MANAN

Fishing boats stroll in and out
of the harbor, gulls ride along
the curvatures of wind, fog herds
its cloud stuff into fishhouse alleys.
The only reason to come here
is to watch the unimportant happen,
to move out of the small world
of what we own—house to cottage
to car to clothes—and make everything
public with an unhurried gaze.

I'm reading about an epileptic
so afflicted his brain had to be
surgically calmed—the hippocampus,
some amygdala and cortex removed—
the side effect, he could no longer
learn a new name, couldn't remember
that his favorite uncle had died.
Each time he heard of the death
he experienced that first high-voltage shock.
Memory must protect us from overload,

as simply as when, the first day back,
we heard of one man's numbing stroke,
a woman's eye lost to bad surgery
(one-eyed she can't trust her footing
to berry the familiar back trails),
and a kid, drunk, who went down
while his friend held onto the flipped canoe—
so much loss we were stunned,
but the next week, acceptance surfacing.
The researchers say that emotion helps us

remember, a gateway to what's stored.
I'll remember, of the three, the one who drowned.
No. The one who watched and held on.
This place is layered with memories
of a more gentle nature.
Now in Whale Cove, where at ten I hiked
the Red Trail with my parents, my wild brother
perched precariously on the cliff's outcropping,
where twenty years later I hiked the Red Trail

with friends, their teenage son perched
precariously on the cliff's outcropping—

the shock value, for me, gone—but the father
laughing in that tense should-I-try-to-stop-him
way, now in Whale Cove a man rows
his mustard-colored dory to the weir,
the darkness of his silhouette
cutting the fog. It may be impossible
to define the borders of a single memory,
to see just one thing. So what does it mean
that I return summer after summer
to a small northern island where I hope

to dwell in a visual calm, as if no mind
would dissolve the scene into memory,
stack it against other events
labelled "Whale Cove," which itself
is a now-seeming past—raw copper melted
into fresh Triassic rocks, basalt columns
rocketing up and fracturing into blocks
to be softened by tides.
Everything is physically changed
by what happens—neurons and islands

popping into a surprise kind of order,
tracks of memory mixed in the moment
until you feel you're driving
past a cornfield that looked like acres
of random tassels and stalks, then
from one point of view the mass breaks up
into rows parallel as a musical staff.
What we own is the ballad of our
own inside story—a place where a man rows,
where no moment is alone with itself.

LETTER TO NATHANIEL HAWTHORNE

It's Sunday
and the yachts wave like handkerchiefs
of bon voyage. Only artists and priests
work on days like today, and vendors
who breeze like sails through the park.
I've wanted to write you since I was twelve,
the year I started to menstruate and Mrs. Gorman
asked in English if I had inherited your talent.
I was so unaware of my own fertility
I felt like she'd handed me a surprise test
on the one chapter I'd read and reread
and still couldn't fathom. I believed
to write what one knew would be insufferably dull
like wearing khaki for the rest of your life.
I didn't yet know how distinct each inner cinema
could be, how the love of language could provide
the most extravagant wardrobe. I read
that you wore a heel-length writing gown.
Sophia sewed it—the purple cloth
offset with a gold palmleaf, red lining.
When the left skirt became black with ink
as large as a hand where you wiped your pen,
she added a butterfly patch. I know
by this sign of your dedication
that you get my drift about Sunday.

The professor who came to the house
to discuss an island we have in common,
recognizing the portraits of you and Sophia,
said she was a socialist and you
a timid jack-a-dandy who never trusted fame.
I'm tired of sifting the shards of your life,
waiting to comb the Italian notebooks
for the incoherence that might suggest
unfinished business I'm meant to take up.
Whose business is ever complete?
Though your loved ones had to hope—
"Our friend finished all that God
gave him to do"—the eulogy sealed with
your unfinished romance, a wreath of apple blossoms
laid on your coffin. Your life, till the last,
was touched by the invisible: two years saw

your hair turn white, handwriting change,
manuscripts speckled from nosebleeds and
the roughly embellished figure "64"
written over and over when nothing else came
as if death had already begun to use you
naming the year it would blow into your sleep.

We've become like the family of steeplejacks
I saw on the news—each generation picking up
the trade because it makes sense to climb
jury-rigged scaffolding. It's work
they don't mind getting up to, although you
accomplished enough to face us
with what more we can become—your Puritan
burning to incorporate the wilderness
beyond his parceled yard, the woodland
so dense his improvised path closed
two feet behind him. Who doesn't want a place
unharmed by hands and wheels, where leafmold
grows into cotyledon, pedicel, and calyx,
and the meaning of generation comes clear.

One inherits too much baggage to ever
step clear of the past. This was plain to you
suffering your great-grandfather,
the Justice who hanged his neighbors
when they denied being witches
and showed none of the signs—vomiting of
nails, bones, and needles—which inspired
carnivals in Europe where hundreds
of the accused were burned while vendors
hawked rosaries to the crowd. In New England
bewitchment was more subtle, execution more refined:
simple hanging by the neck for one Rebecca Nurse
who came a-railing at her neighbor because his pigs
had gotten in her field. The neighbor taken
with fits, struck blind, falling three times
in the doorway, coming to, saw death
sitting at his dining table. When it was done
the husband of Rebecca Nurse was made
to pay the customary fee for hanging.

You read the same accounts and changed
the spelling of your name—how Justice
Hathorne did preside over every hanging

and, though the jurors later published
their "deep sorrow at having acted on such evidence
in condemnation of any person," the name
of our forefather was not among those listed.
How was it possible—his parents had come,
charged with God's will, had dared
the three-month voyage in the grip of fickle weather,
cramped below deck in the shit stench—America was first
the smell of hemlock, ripe gooseberries, swamp roses,
wafting like the din of migrating grackles
off the stone coast. You did accomplish,
if not a pardon, at least a redirection
of the hope for perfection—the tendency,
inherent, of which I hesitate to speak,
not wanting to be dismissed.

The wind is up, white sails flap, flags
of a pacifist nation. From this distance
the yachts seem to move without effort.
At times my life seems touched by the invisible—
when my husband picks a fairy tale to read aloud,
"The Tailor in Heaven," it works like a hexagram
convening my mind. It happens
that a light-fingered old tailor arrives
at Heaven's gate on the day the Lord has gone
to check out the new delphiniums.
St. Peter, a cautious soul, but sympathetic,
knows the old man has snipped cloth away
from his best-dressed, most trusting customers,
but he softens hearing of the tailor's
blisters and lameness from his long journey.

Once inside the gate the tailor forgets
Peter's warning that he should hide
behind the door until God returns.
The tailor snoops through every chamber
of Heaven, finding in one a row of elegant
chairs, one much taller than the rest,
studded with rubies, cast of a higher carat
gold than any found on Earth. The tailor climbs up,
rests his feet on the gold footstool,
sees everything as it happens below:
an old woman washing laundry at the public stream
tucks away two silk veils for herself.
The sight makes the tailor so angry

he grabs the gold footstool from under his feet,
pitches it down at her, then ashamed, scurries to hide.

The Lord returns, having never left,
as only the Divine can do, and calls the tailor
to his feet. "You old fool, if I judged
as you do I would long ago have had no chairs,
benches, not even a knife and fork
to enjoy my supper. And how would you
have escaped so long?" The tailor,
sent to Wait-a-While, for the first time
sees Heaven and Earth as one mansion
built around a thatched cottage heart.

Your way of judging the world,
even at age four, was clear.
The winter your sister gave you
the bust of John Wesley, starched
bib and posture boasting sermons
endless and right, you filled it
with water through a hole in the pedestal
revealing its hollowness, stood the figure
on its head in the cold, waiting
for the juggernaut to freeze and burst.
Paradox came late, when history began
to haunt with—you meant to burst all pretense
by striving for a bigger view. Salvation, never
to be won by faith alone, would flow
from the bronze inkstand on which the infant
Hercules struggled with a goose for its quills.

Once I read a magazine self-help test
designed to cure the perfectionist.
It had me rate various activities—
reading a book, writing a letter,
making love, sewing a skirt—
by the amount of satisfaction
anticipated and realized from each.
I've forgotten exactly how it worked
but I learned that I expected the least
from sewing and therefore got the most.
But what if someone's truth
is a nagging expectation? Then to follow
this mass-market advice is to self-inflict
a wound impossible to heal or die from.

Such a victim burns from inside with guilt
for not going public with what he knows.

                              I'm trying to grasp
why you passed the day writing stories
and the night burning them, why you paced
the ridge at the Wayside until roots
were laid bare, composing in your head
a way to speak in the marketplace
that would lift the veil of goods.

My aunts and uncles, like my parents,
each have one blue china plate that came
packed in a sea-chest with ruffs and linen,
leather and buckles, seeds, sheepskin
and clothes for four years. Passed
through nine generations, these small
ornate dishes did their stint on your table.
Or perhaps you too hung them on the wall
to study their beautiful, unlikely persistence.

Today the future's an overcrowded National Park—
no room for what should last. Still, I learned
what you learned—talk to a dead man
and no one will answer. You find yourself
the only one talking, hoping everyone listens
to keep alive the desire that inhabits
their hearts. Then your turn is over.
You turn into someone's idea of you.
But what you *did,* inventing a democracy
of guilt and pardon, still excites an expectation.
The yachts move without friction. I'm finished
feeling so small I envy their effortless pleasure.
They're just yachts, and there's no place
free of history left for them to go.

THE DREAM OF A MORAL LIFE

Driving north into fields of elk and wild grass,
we left the city's clash and speed behind
to watch three turkey vultures
soar, alert, a mile above
the pool of idling carp.
At dusk a swallow flitted
through the campsite—dips and upswings,
fragments of that hyperactive song.
The Black River ran diamond clear,
facets cut by laser rays of Arizona sun.
Downstream you tried to keep in sight
the single salmon egg
bobbing toward the rapids.
Casting into the unknown,
you like to call the enterprise,
glad the Apache trout and native browns
have grown too smart for your lures.
I flipped my z-ray across a deeper pool—
an artifice of boulders that Fish and Game
with a backhoe (even here!) had made.
We wanted supper and got it.
Two pink-fleshed stockers apiece,
their spangled sides turned crisp
with butter and cornmeal, the campfire
whistling sap out of heartwood,
while we pulled meat clear from the bone.

I failed to sleep that night,
the ground so hard it taught me
a thing or two about my bones.
The moon worked for hours at coming
over the spruce-smudged ridge.
And the water tumbled by sounding
the way the wind had at noon,
humming through the aspens.
Such music can make a single thing of us,
though hours earlier I would have
blamed you, if I had the chance,
that I got busted by a ranger on horseback.
I forgot she didn't have a license,
you admitted to his suede knees,
while I fumbled for my faculty I.D.,
as if my status of employment

could buy his leniency. He smiled down
at you, ghost of the manly protector,
Hey, you can only look out for yourself,
handed me the citation, turned the buckskin's head,
and, as if he were my friend, said,
Don't let it ruin your day,
as if admitting how small a place
the pursuit of happiness leaves
for laws. He clicked the mare forward,
leaving me to sulk and sleep it off
in the afternoon sun, waking up to myself as
good enough, or
bad for good enough reasons, or just
distracted by the music of what was passing by.

— after Gary Young

II

FIRST ENCOUNTER BEACH

Eastham, Massachusetts

One of the spectators is disappointed
there isn't a guide to explain
the beaching, the scientists busy
cutting into ninety-four pilot whales
stranded on the salt grass.
No one knows why and, try as the rescue team
might, not one whale will go back to water.
So they're injected to speed up the dying,

lined up like lumber and sawed into,
except when the black skin splits
we can't stop staring, their meat is so red.
I don't want to know why this happens—
what parasite or geomagnetic anomaly
finished their love of motion. Why should
anything have to leave this world
when water can cycle from atmosphere
down to land, the ocean and back
to forgiving sky.

                    I'm on my way to Connecticut
where my father has a little *vegetation*
on his heart valve—that's how the intern
describes it, trying to minimize
the danger of him slipping
into a haze so cold, some nights,
bone-cold, his hand can't get from
his plate to his mouth.

                    Rain slicks the highway
slowing me down. The same water
fattened into snow in the woods
of my childhood, the whiteness
unbroken except where my father
cut trails and taught me to ski,
laying down herringbone behind him
as he broke up hills that left me
with legs made of slush. He wanted me strong,
no patience for pain. No choice
but to find the muscle to follow. Even now
when he boasts how I zigzagged
the breakneck hills in an icestorm,
there's no hint of my knee-chattering fear,
slats skittering out of control,

each run a victory of luck more than will,
each ride up the lift a prayer for my bones.
I wonder how it is for him now
there in the ward where whiteness can't hide
the cold blank that's ahead. When the whales
beached, spectators came like pilgrims,
each new arrival scanning the faces
of those heading back to their cars
to see how it changed them
to survey so much death. Nothing showed.
Their eyes followed the asphalt,
heads bent in private devotion.

                                    There in a room
where others have died, my father
keeps a record of each test and drug.
He watches medicine drip into his arm
and circle in the dark of his blood.
I believe it will heal him, as I believe
in the strength of my blood
to protect me from failures of will. Once
when my grandmother at ninety-six
lay delirious with pneumonia,
pitching on her high horsehair bed,
she saw three crows perched on the dresser.

They smell so awful, she said.
Please, open the window. Let them out.
It was my father who did what she asked.
And the crows flew out, carrying her fever
over the treeline, dissolving into sky,
and she lived. Whatever she saw,
by love, luck or dumb Yankee will,
it was true. That's what I mean by medicine.

BELLS

Five mornings a week while we hung
at the blond breakfast table,
your radio voice talked us into the day,
telling the time with a wooden bell
carved from the huge Charter Oak

which fell in the hurricane
no one forgets. The press photo
shows you reporting that storm,
making news ripple from the high metal tower
connecting homes through thin air.

Fans sent more bells to the station—the porcelain doll
whose double clapper wore high-button shoes,
a cracked Liberty replica
sent by the Plainville Legionnaires . . .
You were the breakfast in each of their kitchens
until television made radio go stale

and the bells came home, filling a wall
it was my job to dust. I cleared the mahogany
shelves one by one, letting the bells
wag their tongues—the monkey wearing a tasseled fez,
the bronze crane whose clapper
hung like an eel from its beak,
and the train of African elephant bells—
lime-size treble to cantaloupe bass.

There was one crystal bell
with a ruby glass handle that had no tongue
and didn't ring, just waited
to be broken. I never thought
before today to tell you
how scared I was of a thing so fragile,

how much I loved the sound
it could have made, as if all the times
I couldn't think of what to say
would find release if I could make
that thin glass ring.

—for my father

BREADING THE SOFT-SHELLED CRABS

I have neglected my body,
working myself into a shell
so that, breezing into the fish market today
and seeing the delicacy I had long forgotten
set apart from the usual mussels and sole,
I might be eight years old

out to eat with my parents at Johnny's Restaurant
and able to order anything I want.
Even now, breading the soft-shelled crabs,
their finely stippled bodies that give to the touch,
translucent as Japanese lanterns,

I sense how thin is the membrane
between what I was and what I long to become—
both states of the shell
as it hardens and sloughs,
hardens and sloughs as the season demands.

AT THE HAIRDRESSER'S I THINK OF HERACLITUS

In high school I played the ingenue—
hair done in a sideswept bouffant
as immovable as baked meringue—
trying to keep that style,

teasing and spraying, molding
the flyaway ends. Later I taught
language to a child wasted on silence,
spelling out W-A-T-E-R, wrestling

the knowledge into her hands—
my hairstyle severe, pulled back
straight to the brain stem.
Now with no part, I ask for a trim

eager to watch the curl bounce back
and I think Heraclitus should have used hair
instead of the river—these follicles
streaming with unmanageable growth

I try to contain with a new style—
each cell a tiny model of the soul
growing by the logos of its need
so that the hairdresser
never cuts the same hair twice.

EVE REVISITED

Pomegranates fell from the trees
in our sleep. If we stayed
in the sun too long
there were aloes
to cool the burn.
Henbane for predators
and succulents when the rain was scarce.

There was no glorified past
to point the way
true and natural
for the sexes to meet.
He kept looking to the heavens
as if the answer were anywhere
but here. I was so bored
with our goodness
I couldn't suck the juice
from one more pear.

It's *here,* I kept telling him,
here, rooted in the soil
like every other tree
you know. And I wove us
a bed of its uppermost branches.

DREAMWORK

The elders wear black robes. A woman with grey hair
kisses me. I'm reserved, give a peck. She kisses
me again. I'm the same. Again—it isn't passion
she wants from me, but simple connection unobstructed

by fear. My assignment is *Oil and Thunder*. I'm
instructed to go first. I'm angry, this is unfair,
I've never been here before, others are more experienced.
The judges watch me. I have no choice but to begin.

"When I first understood the relationship between
oil and thunder, I was mediating conflicting claims
between a foreign mining company and a small town
in northern Vermont." As I tell the story

I'm aware that my mind's on a double track:
one tells the story, while the other thinks ahead,
afraid the judges can sense my inner tangle,
amazed it comes out so clear, so neatly woven.

But I go on too long. The judges are restless,
my children pace by the doorway, point to the clock,
make me read lips: "We'll be late for our curfew."
But I can't help it. I have to complete

the story in spite of them. "The relationship between
oil and thunder is power. Oil is expendable,
a limited commodity, a production of reduction. Thunder's
the greater power, self-renewing, an invisible

collision of heavenly forces, a process
only hinted at by reverberating earthly sound."
The room is quiet. The children wait,
scanning the elders for a sign of conviction.

FROM AWAY

My friends describe the perception of children—
how one might say, *the moon follows me home,*
or hold regular phone calls with a reindeer.

And the best teacher says, *yes,* believing
wrong answers are right for that age. Later,
in bed alone, missing the bow of your legs

against mine, I imagine myself even farther away
living on brandy and radishes, so far
from back roads that only a misguided hunter

stops by asking the way back home.
I show him my Toggenburg goat, bitter milk,
and the pigweed that grows wild for my kitchen.

My patience has grown so perfect, I tell him,
that partridge you see hanging over the sink —
I sat like a stone for three days by its nest

and it walked right into my hands. Upstairs
my friends make love, while through my open window
comes a pulse from Venus and I remember

myself, waiting for sleep, opening possibilities
like windows on an advent calendar.

STUCK FOR REPAIRS IN TUCSON

He bought pigeons after divorce,
attaching a band to one ankle of each,
and taught them to home from Phoenix
then Vegas, timing their return—
the second they fold their wings he scores.

He claims the prettiest,
necks checked with mother-of-pearl,
are slower, their sonar more easily scrambled
by hawks or wind over Grand Canyon,
their wings giving in to the current.

Birds circle over his house,
a lariat that responds to his hand.
He misses the one who hasn't come back
after thirty-nine days, one
who must have learned to feed herself.

He checks off the days she's been gone
on an oversized calendar of nudes.
June veils her breasts with fuschia, July
slides green silk between her thighs,
and August turns her blue back.

THE MASSAGE

At work it's called *massaging the data*
when the sealed files of childhood
are opened to determine
how old the mothers were
when they gave their babies away,
as if age could tell you something
about love or fear or inadequacy.
I'm almost forty, complained my lover,
as if by now he should know
what he wants, instead of saying,
I can't see you anymore,
then making fantastic love.

Later it's someone else's work
to find the seam
at the base of my skull
where questions harden
into knots. It's called *carrying*
in the lingo of bodywork,
as if I were pregnant with tension,
an embryo misplaced in my neck
so I never could love it enough.
Undo me, I tell him, the one
whose hands let me
give my arms away one at a time.

SATURDAY, J.'S OYSTER BAR

Hearing there's no lemon pie,
the businessman orders more oysters
cracking nautical jokes—*There will be liberty,
but not boats*—his gestures formal
as the crest on his blazer.

The waitress, buying the proprietor's
idea of provocative, wears black pantyhose
and burgundy short-shorts. She's never heard
of sherry, so she brings me something
sweet and red as I settle into the notebook

to add to my letter of this morning.
I'm not like you, celebrating marriage
with goat cheese and basil, red tulips
and champagne. On Saturday I go out alone
looking for the city to dish out

its bucket of steamers, shells
the color of rain that stipples the alley
where pleasure boats tip at their moorings
exaggerating the pitch of the storm. I pry open

the shells, swish the clams in broth
and love the near hour it takes me
to work through the tin. *Sierra Club*
it reads when I get to the bottom,
as if I'd just hiked up the Panther Trail

past knee-high yellow trumpet flowers
that out-blare the bees to camp at the summit,
look out on houses each corralled by its lawn,
where white smoke lifts from two chimneys
five miles apart, gunshots rise from the gravelpit.

Inside those houses women set tables
with linen, crystal and pears,
while I look in from the woods, think
theirs is the wilderness that can't be tamed.

—for Suzanne Levine

SHAKERS

East of Albany there's a starkness in November,
the grey crewcut of trees rounding hills
called the burned-over district for the fires
of spirit revival that swept over them and out.

I haven't driven this road since the summers
I worked at Shaker Village teaching teenagers
to reproduce—*hands to work, hearts to God*—
the original flat brooms, oval boxes, song

and trembling of the life without sex that filled
those god-sized houses—two doors, two stairways
to keep clear the line between the old carnal nature
and the mission above. I had a lover there

and we argued. Though I didn't trust his nervous hands,
trembling when he smoked, or the Monte Carlo way
he drove his Peugeot, some days it was enough
to spin off to town, rent a cheap room,

get steamed and satisfied, then drive back,
calm as if we'd been to a staff meeting
at which no issues were raised. I don't know why
I held back from loving him, but he did the same.

I don't blame it on sex, though in that context,
we couldn't help asking if community
cost a price we weren't willing to pay.
For us, spirit meant loving the body

and, though we owed the Shaker ghosts for our paychecks
those summers, we only earned them with manual tasks—
make it so it lasts a thousand years.
I'm as sorry I was never ready to love him

as I am that love failed the craftsman
who buried his poem in the wood shavings
stuffing a leather shop stool—
June 30, 1871. To the finder. Remember me.

It's good to see these hills roll up and down,
granite outcrops like high foreheads, good
to think of fires flared here and spent
for any uneasy truce between body and soul.

RECEPTION
variation on a line by Czeslaw Milosz

How awkward can you get, I think,
sinking into the vinyl chair
to finish my lemonade and vodka.
I still feel twelve at receptions
where strangers make talk smaller
than the shaved ice disappearing
in my plastic cup. Oh for a friend
who would tell me her peas and onions
are in, or did I notice the arteries
on the ankle of that woman in red.
But no, it's always the same.
Clever talkers hustle the guest of honor,
hoping to catch a dose of the fame,
and I lurk by the punchbowl, think
how stupid to say, "You are the shine,
the juice, the rouge of the day." But if I
were on stage, a handshake from the woman
with receptive eyes would signal
connection enough to feel the labor
worthwhile. So this is for everyone
I never told how much they meant to me.
On second thought, this is for you,
my self-contained child, too shy to speak
without filter of friends. You can go
to bed now. There's a grown-up in the house.

SNAPSHOTS FOR MY DAUGHTER

You were five I think when we watched the cat
chase her backside under the bed
and let out a wail sharp as a bandsaw
as the first slick lump emerged.
The cord intact, she circled and circled,

and for seconds we felt the panic
she wouldn't know what to do. Then
she licked away the sac, freed the paws
to reach with inborn instructions for warmth.
You said, It wants to go back.

Nine summers later I packed you for boarding school.
You practiced walk-overs in the yard, demanding,
Watch this, hey, watch! As if I could miss
the sleight of your body, breasts rising
like trick doves, the chest

I could blanket with one hand
gone for life. That summer we recovered
two iron wheels left for rubbish
by the farmer before us. We hooped them home
through the hayfield greening for a second cut

and stood them on the porch,
as if they might signify
we were ready to let go. I never felt more helpless
than when you called from Mexico, homesick,
the trip a present for your sixteenth birthday.

I gave you what you needed but I couldn't
make it easy. That night I dreamed
I carried a baby so small
the birth was painless, but the deeper rip
where the blood-lace last connected us
ached a long while into morning.

SCENES FROM A CHILDHOOD

How We Did It

The snowbanks rose taller than the car,
a midnight bobsled run, our ride home—
you asleep under parka and quilt,
home from the sitter, me from the failing

ski resort where the married chef
hustled me nightly, while I shoved
steaming racks of dishes along
the stainless steel drainboard.

The sitter's husband too came on to me,
a wiry deadbeat, metal pin in his leg
from some war. He told me how it
held the cold, taught me to pound

cornmeal and molasses sweet grain
from the freight car walls,
the bunch of us climbing with sacks
up to the backlot siding

where the rusty hulks stood
after unloading at the Richford mill—
free feed for the hogs and hens
you hated me for butchering.

Those were the improvised years
after King and the Kennedys—hopes
humbled down to living with the powerless—
flocks of us, exurbanites, trying to invent

community in the impoverished north
where abandoned shells of homes
lay scattered over hills
as if some sea had backed out and left them there.

Is there a placeless place you came from,
as mystics tell us, where souls drift
inspecting the candidates
they might elect to bring them here?

Those icy mornings in our ramshackle,
wind welcoming house, you twirled on a swing

that hung in the kitchen doorway, singing like the necessary
heat rising from the cast iron stove.

Seven

She got through the surgery,
came home with a bitter drug
lodged in a place my maternal
pep-talks couldn't touch.

Days of that. Maybe weeks.
Then, her lounging in the leggy grass
beside the vegetable garden
while I hauled water in the milk-can,

forked the meadow sod, foot by square foot,
dragging feed sacks of manure
across that bird-haven hard scrabble farm.
What broke the peace between us

I don't remember. But there in the open
it blew. Both of us screaming, in tears,
down to the rawness that comes
from family love, the red-faced embarrassment

of anger as it bakes out of the body
what can't be said at normal temperature.
Her accusation: *Why didn't you tell me
the truth? I knew I could die.* Spiraling through

my own first awareness, the night terrors, lying
awake with the light on as if death
could only see in the dark—I saw that
I had no faith to protect her

as none had protected me. We turned suddenly
from that intensity, and there
in our pasture miles from any house but our own
stood a man watching, holding a battered bicycle—

not a man, a boy in man's body, big-headed,
riveted to our fighting
there in the rutted high grass.
We all stared at the silence, terrified then,

not by our deaths, but by our lives, and he smiled,
this being who would go on smiling at all the wrong times—
a figure of our own ignorance and wonder,
turning his bicycle in the weeds, teetering away.

Alliance, Ohio

A funky campground five miles into corn rippling farmland.
Japanese lanterns strung down by the pond
where a party spills into the night. *Just the two of you?*
asks the gatekeeper, *aren't you afraid?* stepping from his trailer

with pliers in hand. *Car trouble?* he asks, too nice, we both think.
You give me your best let's-get-the-hell-out-of-here look
while the repressed fundamentalist leans under our hood.
He thinks we're friends, not mother and daughter—

a mistake common in your teens, my thirties. Guys
in their twenties trying to pick us both up.
This one tells us to park near his trailer,
in case there's an emergency. And . . . uh . . .

leaning close like he's my favorite uncle,
Don't go to that dealer. He'll see you coming
with those Vermont plates. Just buy a case of oil
and a funnel and you'll make it to Yellowstone.

I was a fool, I think, to say we're headed west,
no one expects us for a month. Should have said
our sister in Toledo expects us tomorrow. He watches TV
until the other campers' lights are out. You want to leave,

sure he's the emergency to come. *Don't worry,*
I assure, *if he comes back here I know what to say.*
Just go to sleep. I lie awake, the camp hatchet
in my palm under the sleeping bag, reciting my best

prayer against breakdown, prayer against storms,
against psychopaths, prayer for the sanctity of motherhood.
You're already asleep. Listening hard for footsteps,
I hear trees creak against the wind all night.

Museum Piece

You didn't like yourself for crying
the day a child came to the museum
strapped to a wheelchair, helmeted,
punching her head, eeking proto-words

out of the argument with herself,
herself the thing from which
she needed protection. On break,
the other security guards chatted over coffee,

and you wished you too could banish
your feelings into the exile of boredom.
You frightened me that year, twenty-one,
leaving college to play with the Gorehounds

and the Brood in that cellar bar
where punks and junkies bellowed out
mean tunes. You'd leave the house at 10 P.M.,
skin molded in black, a silver crucifix

aimed at your crotch—that chain a woman
should know would lead her to pay.
I taught you this—never be ashamed.
And though I feared I would witness

the elegy of my success—squandered,
the legacy of my experimental life—I kept the homilies
coming, hoping they'd prove true—we learn
our strengths by living through hard things.

The Pelican

The velvet black mane on its broken neck
the skin sack accordioned up against its monstrous beak
the red smear on its cartilage lips
the claw at the tip of its beak
the black leather webbing of its feet
the zagged wings, black stylus pin feather
the white quills, the span wide as a sidewalk

Fresh dead, it flexes and droops to the touch—only the eyes
have been pillaged, the body incorrupt
(that old word of relics and saints fitting its grace)

We had walked miles after sunning in plastic chairs
what's that thing? a dead gull? a ripped tire?
we asked before heading off down the sand
trying to find the story of your grandmother
(briefly my mother-in-law) who drowned in a lake
while the tinsel conversation of a dinner party
filtered down into silence, evening mist

All we could find were versions of the story—
medication and shock replacing her memories
with blanks—was she deranged or sanely
enraged at her husband's infidelity
when she set their bedroom on fire and walkedπ
in her nightgown down Harris Road? what if
she had lived now when marriage is a question
which a woman can ask, answer, make fun of, or ignore?

Returning to the place we'd started from
our notebooks, sunscreen, and towels
still strewn beside our plastic chairs
we walked up to the thing we hadn't
gotten close enough to
to name—

Creature who lived without love—though what
is flight but the body in love
with its motion, its marriage to air? without words—
though what is this chin-sack, this gathering bag,
this receptacle which opens to fill its fish-stench cavity
but a language in which there is no past or future tense
only to be to be to be to become

III

What it takes to dazzle us, masters of dazzle,
all of us here together at the top of the world,
is a night without neon or mercury lamps.
Black sheen flowing above,
the stars, unnamed and disorderly—
diamonds, a ruby or sapphire,
scattered and made
more precious for being cut
from whatever strand
once held them together.
The universe is emptiness and dust,
occasional collisions, collapsing zones of gas,
electrical bursts, and us.

Here is the 60-inch scope where
we struggle to see one pinpoint of light,
each singularity with its timid twinkle
become a city of stars, that trapezoidal
grouping at the end of Orion's sword,
a cloudy nursery spawning
galactic stuff, lit but not illuminated
by a glassy hot blue star. What is it to see?
A mechanism wired in the brain
that leads to wonder. What is it
to wonder but to say
what we've seen and, having said it,
need to see farther.

Here are the globulars and spirals,
the dumbbell, ring, and crab—particles
swept like water in a drain, shapes
mapping the torque that shapes them,
tension of matter, micro- and
macro-scopic, orbiting, electron
and planet straining at apogee
like a husky on the leash.
Here is Pegasus, the Great Square—
call it the Baseball Diamond, a story
we can see, one we can use
to find our way back. A scientist
can say *NGC 5194/5* to another
and the other says *Ahhh,*
picturing the massive whirlpool, its
small companion galaxy eddying by its side.

Call it the Nipple with a nearby Mole,
call it the Chief Executive Officer
walking his Spitz. Describing *is* imagining—
knowing, not knowing but
having the language
to convey, to *be* the water carrier,
Aquarius, to quench another.
I saw it with my own eyes.
Seeing is believing.
That paloverde tree is green.
On earth as it is in heaven.
But the sky is not blue
and the stars are not a drifting dome,
merely coordinates plotted on
the immensity inside—
the Eternity we walk in when we dream.

Still the universe (the way we see it)
is more real than Heraclitus,
who said the stars were solid bowls
filled with fire, fire which feeds
on the ocean's watery breath.
Why not, since water is consumed
by fire, imagine it as food?
Why not think the brain's
favorite food is seeing?
We still don't know what light is.
Where matter comes from. How the dust
became fire. Why our fire must
turn to dust. And all we have to go on
(refining the instrument) is our selves—
the skin at the tips of our fingers.

All we have to go on is ignorance—
to pay attention to what we've missed.
tides? Amorph —
one scientist's notation in
The Atlas of Galaxies
beneath a shapeless smudge.
They have to take it seriously, everything
they see, trying to invent
a way to pass it on. In this
they are poets as much as
the visitor who says,
Ohhh, a shooting star,
after she's been told

nothing is burning, nothing shooting,
merely molecules of sky jumping
as dust from beyond whizzes by.
Here is the world's biggest mirror—

a million dollars to cast
the glass in hexagonal molds,
to spin the gleaming saucer
parabolic, then a computer
to cool it cell by cell—
six weeks of that and then another
million, two years to polish
the surface to digital perfection.
Here are those gods and goddesses
seen for what they are—battered rock
and frigid gas, sulfur boiling out
into murderous air—
all of us here together
watching from our blue oasis,
whirling in a frozen fading night
where there is not enough
matter to explain why any of it
is here.

Consider the moon. A fault
visible tonight near the terminator
looks like a crease in fresh plaster.
Sea of Rains, Ocean of Storms.
But it has never been moist,
never felt dew or rivers.
Marsh of Sleep, Sea of Ingenuity—
a map of our misunderstanding.
The wonder is we still can see
the way it pours liquid pearl
over the earth's dark waters
after we know its windless surface,
that implacable dust the moon travelers said
smelled like cap guns, is cratered
with a wire-braced flag, two lunar jeeps,
and footprints no weather will arrive to erase.

Here is the observatory at 1 A.M.,
white domes humming on the mountain top
like brains, antennae feeling
(a mechanism wired) their way

into the wilderness. They won't explain
a thing about the wealth
of blackberries in Labrador,
or the sleep of velvet bats
hanging in the eaves drugged by the sun.
They won't fix history or touch the places
inside we can't get close to.
Looking up, we just keep falling.
Here are the owls who navigate
in darkness, here the scattered prey.

MY INTENTION

What I look for is never what I find
and what I find is always a moment
which wouldn't have arrived if I hadn't
been distracted, mind pacing
from one thought to another that doesn't connect
until I look on the map for the nearest green patch without roads.
Green for the clarity of things that metabolize
standing in one place. So I call up friends
and we drive up the switchbacks past the scorch of summer

to hike off while the sun finds the next ridge west
and we guess a way back with no trailmarkers,
down into the greener basin, redwoods covered with moss
and the air heavy as canvas left out in the rain.
Oaks shell us with acorns and we go farther down
into the mossy air, the trees bigger than steeples,
so many with cores blackened and hollow from lightning strikes,
but solid above, climbing, hardly tapering, up
toward their supper of light.

But whatever we hiked off starts pouring
back over us, driving back down, laundry or work or the argument
that still hangs in the air. Whatever didn't get finished
is waiting, my drifting distraction, which I had hoped
the day would transform into something I could love.
My friend's neighbor stands in the shadow of his driveway
with binoculars. That's Jupiter, he says, the brightest
it will ever be, its orbit and ours at their closest.
Then he brings out the jury-rigged telescope—

eyepiece from a flea market, shaft of plumber's pipe
mounted on a junked turntable, pivoting
on little squares of Teflon. But the mirror,
the blessed two-hundred-dollar mirror, a simple twelve-inch
Newtonian reflector of no ordinary wonder. . . . There,
he shows us, are the moons of Jupiter, four errant darlings,
one so close to the planet it looks like a blister at 10 o'clock,
casting its shadow at 11. That's when it comes to me,
getting the grey bands at the equator into focus,
that this centering on what drifts was my intention all along.

THE WOMAN PAINTING CRATES

All structure is a manifestation of underlying process.
— *Fritjof Capra*

The day after the physicist speaks
I paint crates frosty berry blue
as if to confirm they are solid

or else to admire their masterful
illusion—there is no solid stuff
in these structures made of particles

no one can touch or stop
from spinning at fierce velocities.
I am mostly empty space

and for an instant the terror
of flying apart rushes through me
like a close call on the interstate.

Even this body, good paint,
which I am finally comfortable riding
is made of nothing but process,

is no different from the crate
or the atoms of hydrogen in this brush.
Once all things could be understood

if broken into smaller pieces.
Now, the physicist tells me, matter
disappears into haloes

of transforming unexpected
connectedness. I am more than
that accidental assembly—

but to say it, is like trying
to copy the curved face of Earth
on a flat map. If I could know

that process of energy in myself
I could know what continues.
But knowing is what I try

to train myself out of,
painting these crates a new color
closer to a certain blue.

ISLAND STARS

Coming home from the island variety show
capped with a copycat Hollywood game,
emcee teasing—What is the one thing your wife
would like most to change about you?—husband
squirming for the answer he thinks she thinks
he'll give, as if it's a joke how hard
we have to try to love, how often families fail,

coming home under the island stars, their light
enhanced by northern isolation, shining so clear
and numerous they scatter toward both horizons,
hiding themselves in clusters we see as peaceful—
did I hesitate, the cottage door held open
as I held Orion's gaze? You went off, an alarm,
seeing into the kitchen—an invader circling,

frenzied, flight pattern jagged with fright.
Coat over head, you yelled, I edged in to guide out
the trespasser, but it dove in combat, dodged and
circled again. What then, but to cut lights, prop open doors
and hope for its sonar to sense—what?—the breeze, night air,
the better light of stars. When it was gone—was it gone?—
the weight hung on, something so small and desperate

for its life in the place we feel most safe. Outside
that creature must tremble as we do
knowing something wild and accidental
can interrupt our peace. Now the stars look
so sharp they pierce the night and the river of milk
runs out. That can scare me into praise—
the terrible beauty of things flying apart.

CAMP TONTOZONA

Today I'm lonely for another species—
for the white pine whose roots
graft to its neighbors,
the grove of singular spires
collective underneath,
the strong siphoning nutrients to the weak.

Today I'm lonely for the agave
whose spined leaves grow
packed into a spike
each one opening to flaunt
the ghost print of leaves
it has pressed against.

It's not the rhapsody
of isolation in the wild
I long for. It's the lesson
of red brome and cheatgrass—
family historians who can't keep a secret.
Thank you for being so frank,

I'd like to whisper to the caliche,
that salty excuse for soil
which refuses to open
for trowel or spade, but says,
Yes, let me have it,
to the rain. Rain and more rain

this winter (year of the world's
re-mapping) sprung the grasses
from decades of burn-out,
the root tangle sprouting and taking
the chlorophyll cure
until the desert became

visual velvet. There were gaps
in the green—arcs and ovals,
fractured grids where nothing
would grow. That's how the map-making grass
unearthed a village
which decades of digging couldn't find.

Handprints on clay walls, blackened
with a century of cooking,

infant buried in the living room
to keep the spirit near—not an elegy,
just a gamble on the future, where now the desert grass
leaves a place where only a story will grow.

DREAMWORK WITH HORSES

Last night I dreamed again about the horse
and for once I knew that what I miss
is not the false arcadia of the family farm
where lambs are born with no blood on their faces,
but something wild and vengeful inside,
ignored, now demanding to be fed.

෨

Weeks pass when I forget the chores
until it comes to me like a siren
that the animal must be dead. I rush back
to the pasture. The horse ambles up,
buzzing her lips in contentment, no thinner
than I left her. It's clear she doesn't need me,
though I'm sick of myself for forgetting.

෨

When the horse comes into my suburban house
it suddenly seems possible to keep her
no matter where I live. I lead her out
the kitchen door for a ride, but, barefoot,
must go back for boots. Her bridle, jury-rigged
baling twine, is too weak to hitch her outside.
So I lead her back up the porch steps, inside,
then out, less afraid of injury than of losing
my connection, the possibility of riding
full-tilt across the hayfield.

෨

Even in my wildest dream the horse comes out on top.
Two horses battle, the stallion knocked out,
then men interceding while the herd grazes nervously nearby—
roan, chestnut, and bay shining most beautifully,
as if groomed and curried by their own aggression.
They ditched the cowboy—the stubbled, hard-denim man
hit the electrified fence, flew into the air like a back-lit cloud.

෨

I spent months trying to solve this dream,
conjuring the troubled adolescent
who raged through a stable stabbing out
the eyes of his passion

for the distortion of civilized love.
What waking does to the dream—
when what I wanted was to remain faithful to its clarity.

OFF-SEASON

At first the day sprawled out,
a beach without footprints. So I walked it.
Waves stained the sand and receded
leaving rock crabs, razor clams or whelks,
depending what floor the tide had swept.

Walking out was all expectation.
Gulls feasted along the tideline
until I got close. How far could I go
disrupting their feeding with my progress
to nowhere? I spotted a cloud-colored flag

mounted on a driftwood pole sunk in sand.
That's my mark, I decided, though what blond
occasion it signified I couldn't decide.
Directions to a party in the dunes?
Lovers leaving a token of their truce? Closer,

I saw how the wind spoke the flag's language,
silk tattering to execute an ideal.
How could something broken look so happy,
I wondered, walking back through the clutter
of gull tracks, easing the new idea home.

THE RUSSIANS

When the Russians speak to Kindle,
my landlady's mongrel shepherd, they stoop
beside the wiregrid fence to work
her favorite spots—rump and side of the neck,
the universal language of canine pleasure.

What they say in the other language,
Kindle understands as I do the colossal
redwood on their side of the fence
where the grey squirrel challenges the black one
over a scavenged walnut, their barking

serious and familiar—they've said it before
but that doesn't stop them from elaborating.
I'd like to think it's how they keep their peace
like hedging spouses who argue their way
back together. The dog leans and the old woman

slips meatscraps through the wire, her hands
like garden tools, or something wiser, reaching
from the years-deep foliage—dense ferns, camellias,
twisting junipers, and the walnut tree
with its green packets of trouble. All these years

and their clothes are still Russian—his brimless
embroidered Bohemian cap, her rugged skirt and babushka.
They have made a forest of their own in the city,
this part of their language is clear. No one
who has seen them can believe the world is in danger.

INSTRUCTIONS ON, *OR RATHER,*
EXAMPLES OF HOW TO LOVE THE EARTH

Alaska. Beneath the Chugach Range,
a field ablaze with fireweed.
A couple has come here from the yellow
smog belt of California after losing
their son, a graduate student found
on the cindered running track,
unidentified until someone
found a key tucked in his shoe.
Even then, it was a while
before they had his name because
the night before his girlfriend
had cut his shoulder-length hair.
What was he like, they asked her,
years later, the question, all they had of him
who was lost without explanation
as if he had been one of the earth's
errors. He was intentional,
she had answered, trying to explain
why he'd had a vasectomy at nineteen.
He believed his life should inflict
no harm. The couple stands on a ridge
overlooking an unbroken expanse of young growth—
black spruce, yellow birch—and lakes
so clear they know they'll never snap
that radiance for their carousel.

❧

When the cosmonaut returns to Earth,
ten months of rolling like as asteroid in orbit,
he cannot be embraced. Without gravity
his bones have grown brittle. He is fit
only to be locked in a capsule
crowded with graphs, dials, and orange Gortex.
There he practices "up" and "down" remembering
the blue jewel he circled, conjugating
new verbs for distance. He believes
the earth is dead, never again
will a lemon ripen, fall haphazardly to the street.

—*after Julio Cortázar*

THE GARDENER

Sugar Ray, my pugilistic snap pea,
Dr. Lamborn's finest variety,
nearly strangles itself with abundance
like the fairy-tale pot spewing
porridge until the village is paved,
doors glued shut with obsessional lava,
and the master must come from the cave
to restore the safely fallow time.
And what in July could stop

Egyptian onions from growing fists
at the tips of their tubular stalks,
those purple bulbs growing even finer
straws of knuckled green until abundance
is too much for the plant which leans,
relieved to give up and incubate
in the leveling rot of winter
through which honeybees will survive
on the meal they now gather

from the upturned yellow lampshades
of zucchini flowers, tea-colored nasturtiums
with mahogany pin-stripes that hustle
to thicken their wall of blossoms,
declaring a peppery sweetness to the gardener
who paces the deeply mulched rows,
making a stand for the good work
of staying alive, the good rain
beading in basins where leaf and stalk join.

—for Roger Swain

RECITAL

My teacher, the minister's wife,
just back from Africa, fixed tea
English-style, with milk not lemon,
served in china cups ringed with violets
that seemed as frivolous as the grace notes
in Mendelssohn's "Spring Song"
which I would never be ready to play.

Two baby-grands stood face to face
like horses flagging flies—wild mustangs
which would bolt as soon as I
folded my skirt under my thighs,
trying to sit at attention
before the regiment of folding chairs
outside the minister's study—

that Africa of books and high thinking
he never left. If only my fingers
could bloom with his zeal—violets in the ear!
But I plunged past each finger-tied mistake,
my foot glued to the *sostenuto* pedal
as if I were weightless and it alone
would hold me to the ground. That year—

a freak accident—a stewardess fell
above our town and the fathers fanned out
in search parties to find her. I needed
the miracle that she'd be alive.
The papers said it was possible—
the plane wasn't that high and the pine trees
might have cushioned her fall. All week they combed

the woods for her and for me it was as if
a faint angel hovered over the minister's house.
I tried hard to concentrate on grace notes,
but couldn't get that they were played
without including them in measured time.
I kept her up there in my mind, her body
banking impossibly on its gentle descent.

THE MAN WHO BECAME A DEER

What little I know
about the man who
became a deer is this—
his feet did not cleave
into hooves, his head
never sprouted antlers,
and the parts that mean
manhood did not thicken
with pelt. Once he wanted
to become an Eskimo,
so he ate raw, rancid meat
and slept on the ground.
But he did not change.
This time he hunted
with a dog who could hear
the gesture of a silent
command and the meat he ate
was dark and fresh
as water from a deep well.
The muscle, the blood,
the hair and the skin
replaced themselves
cell by cell—each one
incorporating the molecules
of deer which he ate
three times a day. And
the deer remained hidden,
disguised as a man
in the perfect camouflage
of his body. Sometimes
in his face his friends
would see a quickness,
in his legs a jitter,
a tensing to leap—
his patience became that
of a browser, his heart
that of a hart, and his brain
which only loses, day after day,
never gains cells, woke up
one winter morning to
the heat of the blood of deer
running through its

pipes like antifreeze.
That's all I know about
the man who became a deer—
and that when he loved a woman
she tasted the forest on his lips.

—*for Dick Nelson*

AT THE MARIN EXHIBIT

If a painter looks long enough
(from 1914, say, to 1933)
the sea off Cape Split
begins to fracture
into simple geometry.
Distance doesn't matter
or the right relationship
of sloop to pine. Only
the rough triangulation of woods
to field to rocky coast—bulldozed
patchwork of teal and green. Then
even the frame begins to reflect
the chisel and foxhair touch and
geometry's lost to movement,
white and turquoise coiling
until ten years later—just marks,
lines, blotches, hardly a line
between sea and sky, just grey.
No weather allows such fogbound
monotony to co-exist with
brash chunks of blue.
Then, in the *Portrait of Roy Wass*
With Apologies, the painter admits
that his subject won't be pleased
by this allegiance to brushstroke
over man. That's art—forgetting
what's real and remembering
the way it feels to move
the hand in nervous telepathy
all the while telling yourself—
What a wonderful thing — seeing.
What a life. That's where *you* come in,
just after surgery, retinas
stitched back in place, images not quite
coalescing. You heard about blind kids
examined in colored rooms—how they
went wild in red, slumped in the blue.
What wavelengths pulsed out
of those pigments, you wondered,
wanting what the painter works to know—
a faithfulness deeper than seeing.

—for Ben Mitchell

SEARCHING FOR THE LOST

A bunch of us were riding back to town in the bed of a pickup,
bouncing through the dunes, sloshing on rutted sand,
when we heard the chopper—everyone excited.
Two teenagers knew the model—a Huey something, the napalm scout—
from replicas they'd built. This one, benevolent white.
And someone said, "It's nice to see one and not have to
be afraid. It's just a toy." Though she didn't mean that—
we could tell from her eyebrows she hated the thing.

Now the chopper repeats its course in front of my window.
Two boats cut grids on the choppy bay, combing, combing.
The blue light turns, a man leans over the bow, orange wetsuit
neck to toe. He's ready to dive, though by now the wreck's
been pulled off the breakwater, the buddy taken to shore.
I never thought a helicopter could express a thing
like tenderness—how long and carefully it searched

so that he'd be carried home by human hands,
not dumped out by lowtide. Minutes ago the man
popped open a brew, stood up in the wind and saw granite
replace the dazzle of speed. Now he doesn't feel the wind
pulling everything untethered eastward where the spines
of a broken wharf are stained black by the falling tide.

A diver's flag is up. The drone spills
from afternoon into evening. There must be a science
for conducting a search—the same start-and-halt improvisation
as modeling a molecule's structure. How long does it take
for a lean body to surface? How does wind counter
the drift of the tide? But that's cruel—to think of science
when the night throbs with the death of a young man.

Later I couldn't sleep, the air close. Opened the window
to a heavy breeze, curtains lofting, and I swear I could feel his surprise
to be gone and to be here. I swear I heard a shudder
and a claim—"How come I never thought of this?"
As if he should have seen the place he'd come to
in a preview or an ad. "Look at this, sweet Jesus, hey
look at this." And I said, "Come in here,"
where I was naked for the first night in months.
"You can stay here," I said without saying it, "until it gets quiet."

Of course by then it was quiet. There were windows like that
all along the bayside. He might have blown into every one.

LETTER TO MICHAEL

Last night I dreamed you owned a half dozen dresses,
satin and silk, the bodice emerald green, skirt vermillion,
bands of black and gold. You made me try on the glamour,
though I imagined myself imperfect for the look.
It reminded me of how you once cajoled: "Cut the butch shit,"
when I wore a western shirt and bolo, though we both knew
I wouldn't miss the gender mixing kick of that style.

Michael, all of this is window dressing for what I want to say.
Here the grassy hills ripple off for miles, the patterns of tree growth—
redwoods clustered in the canyons, madrone and live oak thicketing
halfway down the hills—seem random, though I'm told there's history—
lumbering, ranches sold off, land consolidated after the depression—
that's made the landscape so. Who cares, when the vista's beautiful,
at what price or shame the view's been bought.

I remember the days just after the tumor on your arm was excised
and the scans had come back anything but beautiful,
afternoons we collided at the post office and kept walking,
you in a perverse ecstasy (practicing your out-of-body technique?)
that this might be your last spring. How exquisite the fracturing
of the ever-brighter light on the harbor, how miraculous that
just this once the crocuses would cut through winter's crap to bloom.

I don't suppose it will help you when the panics hit to know
I've spun down that linear accelerator myself, though never so
close to impact as you have been now. Years I detested
the lie of childhood—the body grows bigger and stronger, you get A's
and star in the play—promises, promises—while death drums its fingers
in the wings. It's the flavor of loving the mind, which seems to ask
and receive without end, which I cannot abide ever losing.

The new thinking suggests I send images. Voracious shrews consuming
twenty times their weight each day. Quasars in the bloodstream
emitting high-pitched wails that dematerialize the killer cells.
A master microbial sleuth which identifies the aliens and turns them in
to Immune Central. Take that with your visionary meal of garlic,
mu tea and brown rice. And promise to let fly your finest rage—
nature's an imperialist expanding its ego at your expense.

Michael, in the dream with the dresses you lived in an apartment
which I never knew you had, spacious and bright, a fieldstone fireplace,
altarlike, filling an entire wall. Another man was lying on the sofa, asleep,

or similarly absent. He seemed to be absorbed in being absent,
while you danced with me through the wardrobe of many colors.
I know I'm writing to both of you now, though I'll keep "you" the dancer,
and call the other one "him," the one you have to peel yourself away from.

— for Michael McGuire

STAYING OVER NATURE

In memoriam: Myron Stout (1908–1987)

Even in the last year the wool bathrobe
plastered over his clothes, Greek rug
layered over the knees, flannel capped,
four days of white stubble and skin
grown translucent as parchment,
he had it—the urbanity Robert Frank fixed
in his photo-collage from the fifties,
The 10th Street Painters,
each caught in their various funks
of t-shirt, smoke and smudge,

                           Red Grooms
goofing off, Aristodimus Kaldis,
parade marshall at a Happening,
Oldenburg, Kline, Jan Muller and the rest
disarrayed by their art and matted
around Frank's handwritten homily:
MORE SPIRIT. LESS TASTE. REMEMBER. KEEP GOING.
But Myron wears a recherché herringbone,
collar upturned, behatted (yes, a fedora),
cigarette propped in his lips, a genteel Belmondo,
while he studies something out of the frame.

                           He knew more
about the seven ice ages—now thought to be ten
from cores dug in the ocean floor—
than most know about any seven Presidents.
He'd know about the Presidents too,
or how pepper contributed to the fall
of Rome. A landlocked Darwin
devoted to seeing and never, apparently,
disdaining the intricacies of evolution—
though who could know better
nature's no scenic vista, inventing,
along with asphodels,
the gene that made his retinas
melt away. Was he

                    worse off
than Beethoven, never hearing the Ninth Symphony
performed, who had to be turned in the concert hall
to see the applause? *At least he could work,*
Myron said, on one of the afternoons

he hired me to read for him
in the poverty and hyperactive light
of two Provincetown winters. I wondered then,
still wonder—could he have made a painting by touch alone?

ஃ

Hans Hofmann was the teacher who unlocked
the Provincetown painters. A painting *is* energy—
that's what he taught them
with his primate body, gripful of brushes,
a hulk lunging into canvases
that took names, only the names, from nature—
Equinox, Prey, And out of the caves the night
threw a handful of pale tumbling pigeons.
He called it *staying over nature*
when a painter would stick with landscape
after knowing space
goes clear through the terrain—
the phrase only one of the derailments
from Hofmann's native German. He didn't mean it
to convey contempt for a landscape.
Just that, then, artists believed in science,
the headlong train that promised everything
and everyone was excited about unity.

                         Some things
the mind isn't good at, like trying to picture
the proto-universe—that everything's-nothing
tumble of stars, baboons, and symphonies—
as a speck one billionth the size of a proton.
The mind's better at a fractured view,
though, little satisfied, keeps hunting
for what it can't see. The way Myron would
when the macular degeneration left him
only peripheral sight. He'd lean
over magazine reproductions,
circling close with a convex glass
to gather a series of fragments
he had to imagine into a probable whole.
When I asked could he see me, he turned sideways—
I see a sweater, hair, your knees. And turning—
But this way, I see nothing, a grey blank.

                    He saw nature straight on
when he made the graphite of Tiresias—
the head a featureless black oval

in a field of lead shading,
mouth opening perfectly white,
a pure cry against
the nest of blackness it inhabits.

ᢞ

What we read were magazines, stacks elbow-deep
lining the tables—the ones read, face down underneath,
and facing up, topping each pile, the issues that remained.
A year and a half behind, he wanted to keep up
on all he admired in nature, human and otherwise,
now remembering some lines of Chaucer and the way
to pronounce "holpen" which Chaucerian word
he was surprised to have heard
on a bus in west Texas, now saying,
Oh yes, let's read the one about assassin bugs.

                        He never could get
enough of learning, as if to know the fractured world
well enough were to make it complete.
So we read about the warzone
where insects inject prey with poison
dissolving tissues into soup
they sip through the same syringe.
Still, life seems good at adapting to limits—
Kenya's yellow baboons know when to hightail it
to new groves of acacias
to outpace the hatching of their parasites.
And it was good to Myron
that the parasites too would change
if it meant they'd survive.

ᢞ

Once, reading about the Cro-Magnons—
Myron correcting my pronunciation
back to the French—he scoffed
at the journalist's take
that the late Ice Age people
dressed up with strung seashells,
lion and bear teeth *for social reasons.*
That's not it, he interrupted. *It was because
they found the materials
objects of beauty.* As he did, admiring
their huts of stacked mammoth bones—
ninety-five jawbones balanced on skulls

weaving a herringbone pattern, tusks vaulting over
to frame the pelt-thatched roof,

                              the tallow-scented

twilight they lived in.

&

                    Our afternoons
had an architecture. At four we broke for tea,
came back from whatever story into his darkening room,
a little stunned at how much space there was
outside the reading lamp's reach. We sipped
his smoky tea and I would ask him
about the old parties, who was in love with Marisol,
or what the painters then were reading.

                                        Then.
Always then. Because the past mattered
and the present felt frail as an eggshell.
Once I looked up to find an abalone moon had risen,
its light leaking through the shabby walls,
plastic and masking tape
tightening them against the cold,
risen over the frayed Asian carpets
layered one over the other, the books
zoned by topic throughout the apartment—
classics, atlases and reference, art history,
the westerns and the mysteries.

I caught glimpses of liquid pearl
spreading across the Bay and Myron said
he used to able to tell when the moon was full
but he could no longer. Stepping to the door—
there it was right over his walkway—he craned
sideways—*Yes.* And then we were quiet.

&

Months later. I read about clay
flutes and ocarinas unearthed in Belize
along the foothills of the Mayan Mountains.
Myron would have liked the story—how these ancient
instruments, buried for merciless centuries,
were found, scrubbed up and glued,
and their shapes still remembered
how to channel a breath through chambers
where the air swirls into vortexes

that unwind into a few true notes.
What he would have liked best is how
the music made it back from oblivion,
how the energy one mind gives off to another
is one sweet mystery without end.